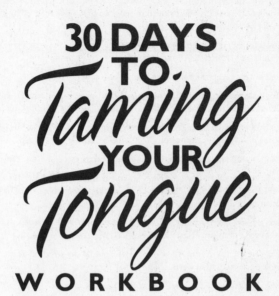

30 DAYS TO
Taming
YOUR
Tongue
WORKBOOK

Deborah Smith Pegues

HARVEST HOUSE PUBLISHERS

EUGENE, OREGON

Cover by Koechel Peterson & Associates, Inc., Minneapolis, Minnesota

Cover photo © Ablestock/Inmagine, Brand X Pictures/Inmagine, Imagestock/Inmagine, Ingram/ Inmagine, Stockbyte/Inmagine, Thinkstock/Inmagine

---

This is a supplemental workbook to *30 Days to Taming Your Tongue* by Deborah Smith Pegues, for those interested in practical individual or group study.

---

30 DAYS TO TAMING YOUR TONGUE WORKBOOK
Copyright © 2007 by Deborah Smith Pegues
Published by Harvest House Publishers
Eugene, Oregon 97402
www.harvesthousepublishers.com

ISBN-13: 978-0-7369-2131-2
ISBN-10: 0-7369-2131-1

Printed in the United States of America

07 08 09 10 11 12 13 14 15 / BP-SK / 12 11 10 9 8 7 6 5 4 3 2 1

Contents

Maximizing Your Study

Congratulations on your decision to go an even higher level of growth in your quest to tame your tongue. This workbook will push you to search the inner recesses of your heart so you can root out impure motives, uncover areas of denial, and deal with other roadblocks that keep your tongue from becoming a wellspring of life. Penetrating questions, thought-provoking Scriptures, and a call for honest introspection will help you build a foundation so the words of your mouth may become acceptable in God's sight at all times.

Because of the level of honesty I am requesting of you, I caution you not to share your workbook with anyone. Treat it as a very personal diary with highly sensitive and confidential information.

Even though this book is set up for daily interaction, take as much time as you need to really delve into the negative uses of the tongue that you find most problematic in your life. Hopefully, not all of them will apply! Therefore, you may find it more effective in your individual study to spend several days on a particular chapter. Notwithstanding, you should prayerfully review the questions and practical exercises in each chapter before you dismiss a single one as irrelevant to you.

Group Study

Even though your answers to some of the questions will be deeply personal, group interaction can be highly beneficial as members share their struggles and provide the spiritual and emotional support necessary to grow.

Each chapter is written on a stand-alone basis, and therefore the material can be covered in any sequence desired. It is my prayer that, as members of a group, each of you will "confess your faults one to another, and pray one for another, that ye may be healed" (James 5:16 KJV).

Writing a Prayer

In several of the chapters, you will be asked to write out a prayer for deliverance. This exercise has a twofold purpose: first, to allow you to acknowledge your need for divine assistance and, second, to give you practice in praying the Scriptures. There are several Scripture verses presented at the end of each chapter that relate to its subject. To the extent possible, make an effort to incorporate these passages into your prayer.

Writing a Personal Proclamation

You will be asked quite frequently to write out a Scripture verse as a personal proclamation. This simply means to personalize a promise or a statement and write it as if it were already your reality. For example, suppose I ask you to write out Proverbs 31:26 as a personal proclamation. The actual Scripture reads, "She opens her mouth with wisdom, and on her tongue is the law of kindness" (NKJV). When you rewrite it as a personal proclamation, you will personalize it by writing, "I open my mouth with wisdom, and on my tongue is the law of kindness."

Personal proclamations are a very powerful faith-building tool that can bring life-changing results. Your faith will be increased as you hear yourself proclaiming God's promises.

Yes, this workbook will show you how to establish God's Word in your heart and how to bring that little unruly member—the tongue—into subjection to the Holy Spirit.

Day 1

The Lying Tongue

Deception takes place when you intentionally try to get someone to believe something you know is not true. It occurs in numerous forms, depending upon the creativity and the desire of the deceiver. God has made it very clear that He has no tolerance for liars.

1. Begin this lesson by reading Day 1, "The Lying Tongue," from your personal copy of *30 Days to Taming Your Tongue*. Note here at least one truth you found beneficial in your quest for a wholesome tongue.

2. List the three categories of lies discussed in this chapter.

    1.

    2.

    3.

- In which category do you find yourself most frequently tempted?

- Which category do you disdain the most in others? Why?

3. List three reasons given in this chapter as to why people often resort to deceitfulness.

   1.

   2.

   3.

4. In the story of Esau and Jacob (Genesis 27), what "benefit" motivated Jacob to trick his father into giving him the blessing of the firstborn?

5. In light of God's word to Rebekah that "the elder shall serve the younger" (Genesis 25:23), what do you think would have been the outcome of Jacob's life had he and his mother not

deceived his father into giving him the blessing that belonged to his older brother, Esau? What lesson can you learn from trying to forcibly obtain your destiny through lies?

6. Do you feel there is ever a justifiable reason for lying?

- If you answered *yes* above, explain under what circumstance. Can you find a biblical reference for your rationale?

- How does your reason above reconcile with Revelation 21:8: "All liars shall have their part in the lake which burns with fire and brimstone, which is the second death" (NKJV)?

7. Recall the last time that you told a "half-truth." What decision or conclusion do you think the hearer would have made had you told him the rest of the facts?

8. Who in your circle of interaction exaggerates frequently, and
    what judgments (if any) have you made about that person's
    character? Be reminded that you yourself may occasionally
    embellish your résumé, the details of an incident, or your
    contribution to a group solution for a problem. We are often
    quick to see the speck in someone else's eye but ignore the
    log in our own.

9. Proverbs 20:7 declares, "The godly walk with integrity; blessed
    are their children after them." Read the story of Gehazi, Eli-
    sha's dishonest servant, in 2 Kings 5:1-27. What impact did
    his lying have upon his future generations?

10. Highlight Psalm 120:2 in your Bible. Write it out below in
    the form of a personal prayer for deliverance from a deceitful
    tongue.

Scriptures to Ponder
for the Lying Tongue

The LORD detests lying lips,
but he delights in men who are truthful.

PROVERBS 12:22 NIV

A man of perverse heart does not prosper;
he whose tongue is deceitful falls into trouble.

PROVERBS 17:20 NIV

Whoever would love life and see good days
must keep his tongue from evil and his lips from deceitful speech.

1 PETER 3:10 NIV

All liars shall have their part in the lake
which burns with fire and brimstone,
which is the second death.

REVELATION 21:8 NKJV

Day 2

The Flattering Tongue

"Flattery will get you everything"—or so goes conventional wisdom. In fact, I watched a television piece produced by a certain network in which they asked bosses and other leaders to state the impact, if any, that flattery had on them. Each one agreed that they indeed had more positive feelings toward those who flattered them and, as a result, were more likely to extend favor to them. It's time for God's children to understand what He has to say about gaining favor in such an insincere manner.

1. Begin this lesson by reading Day 2, "The Flattering Tongue," from your personal copy of *30 Days to Taming Your Tongue*. Note here at least one truth you found beneficial in your quest for a wholesome tongue.

2. Write below the brief definition of flattery as found on page 17 of *30 Days to Taming Your Tongue*.

3. How one responds to flattery is a clear-cut indication of his self-worth. When a person is desperate for affirmation, appreciation, or acceptance, he is most susceptible to being manipulated by flattery—for he gets to hear something wonderful about himself he would love to believe is true. Others, who have a healthy appreciation of their own God-enabled talents and accomplishments, can take the flattery for what it's worth and not be influenced by it.

   Read Acts 12:20-23. Why did the people of Tyre and Sidon need King Herod's support?

   • What flattering words did they use in an attempt to gain his favor?

   • What consequence did King Herod suffer as a result of accepting their flattery as the truth? Why was God's judgment so severe?

4. According to Psalm 5:12, what is the requirement for being surrounded with God's favor?

5. Have you ever engaged in flattery in order to obtain something? Did you receive it? What do you think would have happened had you not flattered the person? What does your action say about your faith in God's promise to supply all of your needs?

6. List two Bible heroes cited in the Day 2 chapter whom God gave favor with others. Summarize below how such favor impacted the lives of others.

   1.

   2.

7. Many women, because of their insecurity about measuring up to society's standard of physical beauty, can become victims of insincere compliments. The model woman in Proverbs 31:18 "perceives that her merchandise is good" (NKJV). Knowing and valuing the intangible assets that you bring to the table is a good safeguard against the deception of flattery. Are you a person who "perceives" (knows inwardly) that your "merchandise is good"? List three of your God-given assets.

   1.

   2.

   3.

Scriptures to Ponder for the Flattering Tongue

A man who flatters his neighbor spreads a net for his feet.

PROVERBS 29:5 NKJV

They speak idly everyone with his neighbor;
with flattering lips and a double heart they speak.
May the LORD cut off all flattering lips.

PSALM 12:2-3 NKJV

Never once did we try to win you with flattery,
as you very well know. And God is our witness
that we were not just pretending to be your friends
so you would give us money!

1 THESSALONIANS 2:5

He who rebukes a man will find more favor
afterward than he who flatters with the tongue.

PROVERBS 28:23 NKJV

Day 3

The Manipulating Tongue

Manipulation is an attempt to subtly influence someone's behavior in order to achieve a desired outcome. Manipulators are masters at exploiting the fears, weaknesses, and insecurities of others. Notwithstanding, their motives are not always purely selfish. Sometimes manipulators have controlling personalities and simply feel that they know what's best for all concerned. They have a hard time accepting the fact that other people have a free will and a right to make good or bad decisions for their lives. They often assert that their intention is to "motivate" rather than "manipulate."

1. Begin this lesson by reading Day 3, "The Manipulating Tongue," from your personal copy of *30 Days to Taming Your Tongue*. Note here at least one truth you found beneficial in your quest for glorifying speech.

2. Manipulators employ various tactics in order to get their way. Some of their behaviors include the following:

- flattering or overcomplimenting
- "kissing up" or ingratiating themselves
- attempting to produce guilt by blaming or shaming
- feigning ignorance of relevant facts
- withholding information
- distorting the truth
- pretending to be hurt emotionally
- appealing to their victim's insecurities or ego
- practicing false humility
- making subtle threats
- crying
- nagging
- hinting or making indirect comments
- using financial enticements
- any other behavior that will tug at the emotions of their victims

From this list, circle the behaviors that you have resorted to in the past.

3. Read Judges 16:4-22. What was Delilah's motive for manipulating Samson into telling her the secret to his great physical strength? What tactics did she use?

4. Recall an incident in which you manipulated someone into taking a certain course of action in order for you to control the outcome of a situation.

   • What was your rationalization for being manipulative?

   • What do you think the outcome would have been had you taken a more direct or godly approach to the situation?

   • Have you repented for this ungodly behavior? If not, write out a short prayer of repentance below.

5. Is there a person in your circle of interaction who tries to manipulate you or your group? What tactics does she use? How do you (or how does the group) respond to her manipulation?

6. Read Luke 20:20-26. List at least two manipulation tactics used by the spies who were sent by the Jewish religious leaders to

trap Jesus into making an incriminating remark about paying taxes to the Roman government. How did Jesus respond?

1.

2.

Scriptures to Ponder for the Manipulative Tongue

Let's just go ahead and be what we were made to be...
Be careful that you don't get bossy;
if you're put in charge, don't manipulate.

ROMANS 12:6-8 MSG

Do you think I speak this strongly in order to manipulate crowds?
Or curry favor with God? Or get popular applause?
If my goal was popularity, I wouldn't bother being Christ's slave.

GALATIANS 1:10 MSG

We refuse to wear masks and play games.
We don't maneuver and manipulate behind the scenes.
And we don't twist God's Word to suit ourselves.
Rather, we keep everything we do and say out in the open,
the whole truth on display, so that those who want
to can see and judge for themselves in the presence of God.

2 CORINTHIANS 4:2 MSG

Day 4

The Hasty Tongue

Words said in haste can ruin relationships at every level of human interaction—professionally, socially, and personally. When we give little or no real thought to our assertions, promises, or proclamations, we set ourselves up for failure, heartache, and regret. Since words can never be recovered, we must take great care in releasing them.

1. Begin this lesson by reading Day 4, "The Hasty Tongue," from your personal copy of *30 Days to Taming Your Tongue*. Note here at least one truth you found beneficial in your quest for a wholesome tongue.

2. Recall the last time that you spoke words you wish you could recall.

   • What negative consequence(s) did you have to face?

- What would have been the outcome had you taken time to consider your words?

- Why did you feel such urgency to speak?

3. Resist being anxious to make your point. Implement a five-second "response delay" rule for responding to anything. Try it for today.

4. Write out James 1:19 below and also on a large piece of paper. Keep it in your sight and meditate upon it throughout the day.

5. Ecclesiastes 5:2 warns, "Do not be quick with your mouth, do not be hasty in your heart to utter anything before God. God is in heaven and you are on earth, so let your words be few" (NIV). Have you ever made a vow to God and later wished you would not have to keep it? Where do you stand on it now?

6. Judges 11:30-40 records the story of Jephthah's rash vow to God in exchange for victory over an enemy nation. Read the passage and discuss how his commitment made in haste impacted his daughter's life.

Scriptures to Ponder for the Hasty Tongue

There is more hope for a fool than
for someone who speaks without thinking.
PROVERBS 29:20

He who answers a matter before he hears it,
it is folly and shame to him.
PROVERBS 18:13 NKJV

My dear brothers, take note of this:
Everyone should be quick to listen,
slow to speak and slow to become angry,
for man's anger does not bring about
the righteous life that God desires.
JAMES 1:19-20 NIV

Hasty Words

How do I take back those words,
Those words I said in haste,
That spewed so quickly from my lips,
Were said in such poor taste?

How do I erase the look
Of hurt upon your face,
And wipe away the tears
That down your cheek begin to race?

I did not think before I spoke,
I did not scrutinize,
Those words that caused you pain and hurt,
I did not realize.

How do I convince you now
I did not mean those words,
When scars upon your heart I left
With words as sharp as swords?

How can I expect you
To forget this thoughtless deed,
When I through angry, hateful words
Did plant a damning seed?

How can I expect you
To forgive my heartless act,
Of speaking without thinking,
And not using any tact?

How do I apologize,
Regain your lost respect?
How do I come up with words?
This hurt I must correct!

The words I'm sorry *seem so lame*
Though what else can I say?
I wish I could take back those words
I said to you today.

Day 5

The Divisive Tongue

Divisiveness is a terrible sin, for it prevents the unity Jesus so ardently prayed for during his final days on earth (see John 17). Further, it thwarts the synergy and effectiveness that results when people work together in harmony. Nothing is more powerful than teamwork in achieving the seemingly impossible.

1. Begin this lesson by reading Day 5, "The Divisive Tongue," from your personal copy of *30 Days to Taming Your Tongue*. Note here at least one truth you found beneficial in your quest for a wholesome tongue.

2. Proverbs 6:16-19 lists seven things that the Lord detests. Note below the three that are committed with the tongue.

   1. haughty eyes   False Witness
   2. Lying tongue   Person Who Stirs up Conflict
   3. hands that Shed innocent blood

   Heart that divises   Wicked Schemes

3. Have you engaged in a divisive act?_____

    • If so, explain below what motivated your behavior (envy, revenge, other).

    • Even if you think it is too late to make amends (assuming you have not already done so), prayerfully consider apologizing for your role in affecting the parties' relationship. Set a time now to speak with each person involved. Record "Mission Accomplished" here when you have completed this task.

4. Have you ever had a relationship ruined because of someone else's divisiveness? Describe the situation and how you responded.

    • What is the current status of that relationship?

    • Is this what you desire it to be? If not, what steps are you willing to take to change it?

5. Do you desire a relationship with a certain individual (co-worker, pastor, teacher, and so on) and find that you envy someone who already enjoys such a relationship with this person? _____ If so, write a brief prayer asking God to deliver you from envy and the "scarcity thinking" that keeps you believing you must compete for a relationship.

6. Are you aware of two or more persons who are in conflict? Ask God to give you the wisdom to play the role of the peace-maker. To begin the process, write below a brief statement of what you would say to each of the feuding parties. Remember to be caring and unbiased.

7. According to Jude 19, what is the underlying reason that a person stirs up arguments and creates division?

Scriptures to Ponder
for the Divisive Tongue

Angry people stir up a lot of discord;
the intemperate stir up trouble.

PROVERBS 29:22 MSG

Always keep yourselves united in the Holy Spirit,
and bind yourselves together with peace.

EPHESIANS 4:3

All of you should be of one mind,
full of sympathy toward each other,
loving one another with tender
hearts and humble minds.

1 PETER 3:8

Those who are peacemakers will plant
seeds of peace and reap a harvest of goodness.

JAMES 3:18

Day 6

The Argumentative Tongue

One quarrelsome person can impact the peace and effectiveness of an entire group. His contentiousness arises from a selfish, unchecked ego that fails to respect the opinion of others and that thrives on displaying intellectual superiority.

1. Begin this lesson by reading Day 6, "The Argumentative Tongue," from your personal copy of *30 Days to Taming Your Tongue*. Note here at least one truth you found beneficial in your quest for a wholesome tongue.

2. Paul admonishes us in 2 Timothy 2:23-25,

> Again I say, don't get involved in foolish, ignorant arguments that only start fights. The Lord's servants must not quarrel but must be kind to everyone. They must be able to teach effectively and be patient with difficult people. They should gently teach those who oppose the truth. Perhaps God will change those people's hearts, and they will believe the truth.

• Write out in your own words the approach and attitude that Paul is suggesting for dealing with a quarreler.

• Describe how you normally respond to a contentious person.

3. Based upon the discussion in the book, explain why some people are argumentative.

4. If you tend to be quarrelsome, what do you think is your root cause?

5. Some churchgoers have denominational pride. They feel that their organization has cornered the market on God's truth and is the only group totally acceptable to Him. Explain your feelings (or lack thereof) regarding the superiority of your denomination (or non-denomination) when compared to related groups.

6. Do you believe there are any church denominations or sects whose followers will be barred from heaven? Explain why or why not.

7. In Jude 3, the early Christians were exhorted to "contend earnestly for the faith which was once for all delivered to the saints" (NKJV). Explain the difference between contending for the faith and being contentious about the faith.

8. What subject matter do you find yourself arguing about most frequently? Does your stance on this matter have a clear biblical basis, or could it be a matter of your personal interpretation? Explain.

9. Will Rogers, the actor and social commentator, asserted that people's minds are changed through observation and not through argument. Do you argue your point of view regarding the matter in the question above with a genuine desire to help the hearer to embrace a critical truth—or to prove your knowledge of the subject?

10. Using Proverbs 20:3 and 17:19 as your foundation, write out a short prayer asking God to give you the wisdom to know when and how to put forth your convictions without being quarrelsome.

Scriptures to Ponder for the Argumentative Tongue

Fools get into constant quarrels;
they are asking for a beating.
PROVERBS 18:6

It's harder to make amends with an offended friend
than to capture a fortified city. Arguments separate friends
like a gate locked with iron bars.
PROVERBS 18:19

The start of a quarrel is like a leak in a dam,
so stop it before it bursts.
PROVERBS 17:14 MSG

Avoiding a fight is a mark of honor;
only fools insist on quarreling.
PROVERBS 20:3

Day 7

The Boasting Tongue

People who boast are on a collision course with the wrath of God, for they believe they are personally responsible for their achievements or good fortune. Their self-exaltation steals God's glory and sets them up for a great fall.

1. Begin this lesson by reading Day 7, "The Boasting Tongue," from your personal copy of *30 Days to Taming Your Tongue*. Note here at least one truth you found beneficial in your quest for a wholesome tongue.

2. What accomplishment has brought you the most praise and recognition? Can you admit to finding subtle ways to let others know about it?

3. When you consider your success, to what extent have you battled pride? What exactly did or do you do to keep it out of your life?

4. Read Gideon's story in the sixth and seventh chapters of Judges. What reason did God give Gideon (Judges 7:2) for reducing the size of his already limited army when he was about to go into battle?

5. Why do you think that man's self-confidence and reliance on his own strength is so repulsive to God?

6. Read Daniel 4:28-37. According to King Nebuchadnezzar, how does God deal with those who boast and walk in pride? Write verse 37 here and on a separate sheet. Meditate on it throughout the day. Memorize it.

7. In 1 Corinthians 4:7 Paul puts our success and accomplishments in perspective:

> Who makes you different from anyone else? What do you have that you did not receive? And if you did receive it, why do you boast as though you did not? (NIV).

Rewrite this passage below in the form of a personal declaration and acknowledgment of God's role in all achievements.

8. Read Esther 5:11-12 and list below the five things that Haman boasted about to his friends.

1.

2.

3.

4.

5.

Scriptures to Ponder for the Boasting Tongue

*When people boast about themselves,
it doesn't count for much.
But when the Lord commends someone,
that's different!*

2 CORINTHIANS 10:18

*People who boast of their wealth don't
understand that they will die like the animals.*

PSALM 49:20

*Do not boast about tomorrow,
for you do not know what a day may bring forth.
Let another man praise you,
and not your own mouth;
a stranger, and not your own lips.*

PROVERBS 27:1-2 NKJV

Day 8

The Self-Deprecating Tongue

Some who engage in self put-downs believe their behavior is a sign of humility. Others fail to realize that *everyone* is inadequate in his own strength and can do nothing apart from the power of God. The self-deprecating mind-set raises God's righteous indignation, because He stands ready to show Himself strong on behalf of those whose hearts are completely focused on Him (2 Chronicles 16:9).

1. Begin this lesson by reading Day 8, "The Self-Deprecating Tongue," from your personal copy of *30 Days to Taming Your Tongue*. Note here at least one truth you found beneficial in your quest for a wholesome tongue.

2. Read the following passages and list the weakness or limitation expressed by each of the biblical heroes indicated when God called them to actions that were completely outside of their comfort zones.

- Moses (Exodus 4:10-11):

- Gideon (Judges 6:11-16):

- Jeremiah (Jeremiah 1:4-7):

3. Describe one of your own perceived limitations that has kept you feeling inadequate or unqualified to pursue a certain endeavor.

4. Write a brief statement of what you would have done by now if this limitation did not exist. Ask God for the courage to step out of the boat and to pursue your destiny.

5. If you could change one aspect of your physical being, what would it be?

6. Explain your understanding of the difference between humility and self-deprecation.

7. What negative label has someone imposed upon you that you have accepted as the *truth?*

8. What negative label has someone tried to impose upon you that you have *rejected?*

Scriptures to Ponder
for the Self-Deprecating Tongue

I can do all things through Christ who strengthens me.

PHILIPPIANS 4:13 NKJV

*Now glory be to God, who by his mighty power at work
within us is able to do far more than we would ever dare to
ask or even dream of—infinitely beyond our highest prayers,
desires, thoughts, or hopes.*

EPHESIANS 3:20 TLB

*God is able to make all grace abound to you,
so that in all things at all times, having all that you need,
you will abound in every good work.*

2 CORINTHIANS 9:8 NIV

Day 9

The Slandering Tongue

Most people do not understand that when they defame the character of another, it diminishes their own character. God hates the slandering tongue and has promised to deal severely with those who engage in such image assassination.

1. Begin this lesson by reading Day 9, "The Slandering Tongue," from your personal copy of *30 Days to Taming Your Tongue*. Note here at least one truth you found beneficial in your quest for a wholesome tongue.

2. According to Psalm 15:1-3, what six categories of people will dwell in the Lord's sanctuary?

   1.

   2.

3.

4.

5.

6.

3. Read 3 John 1:9-12. What actions did Diotrephes, the New Testament leader, take to thwart the apostles from speaking at his church? What insecurity motivated his behavior (verse 9)?

4. Have you ever initiated or taken part in an effort to defame someone's character? If so, what motivated you to participate in this ungodly act?

5. In Proverbs 30:10, Solomon warns, "Never slander a person to his employer." If you observed an employee being maligned to his boss, what steps would you take—if any—to set the record straight?

6. Have you ever been slandered? What does 1 Peter 3:15-17 say about how you should respond?

*Scriptures to Ponder
for the Slandering Tongue*

*He who conceals his hatred has lying lips,
whoever spreads slander is a fool.*
PROVERBS 10:18 NIV

*Get rid of all bitterness, rage, anger,
harsh words, and slander,
as well as all types of malicious behavior.
Instead, be kind to each other, tenderhearted,
forgiving one another,
just as God through Christ has forgiven you.*
EPHESIANS 4:31-32

*Teach the older women to be reverent in the way they live,
not to be slanderers or addicted to much wine,
but to teach what is good.*
TITUS 2:3 NIV

Day 10

The Gossiping Tongue

When we engage in gossip, we run the risk of damaging our own credibility. Credibility is earned over time, but it can be destroyed in an instant. The level of credibility we have determines the extent to which a boss, client, co-worker, relative, friend, or someone else in our circle of interaction will trust us with information or higher levels of responsibility.

1. Begin this lesson by reading Day 10, "The Gossiping Tongue," from your personal copy of *30 Days to Taming Your Tongue*. Note here at least one truth you found beneficial in your quest for a wholesome tongue.

2. Recall the last time you gossiped about someone. Did you initiate the conversation, or did you allow yourself to be drawn in at someone else's prompting?

   • "Gossip is a dainty morsel eaten with great relish" (Proverbs 26:22 TLB). While gossip is idle talk about the affairs of another, it is not always malicious; sometimes people genuinely care about the people they discuss with others and want to know more about them. Why did you desire the information that you received about someone else during the course of your gossiping? Did you have a sincere interest in that person's life? Do you have or do you desire a special relationship with him or her? If so, why didn't you get your input firsthand by talking directly with the person? Respond here.

- Regardless of who initiated the conversation, how did you feel knowing that you were violating God's Word?

3. If you are serious about eliminating gossip from your life, you must cut it off at the pass. When you hear it coming, start looking for a way of escape. Review the suggested responses below and make it a point to implement at least one of them each day.

- "I think we'd better wait until Susie can be here in person to talk about this. I'd hate to draw the wrong conclusion without getting her feedback on the matter."

- "Does John know you're sharing this information with me?"

- "Did Betty ask you to tell me what you're about to share?"

- "Can I quote you when I let Jean and Marvin know we've had this conversation?"

- "I'm going to get in trouble with God if we continue this discussion."

4. Proverbs 20:19 warns, "A gossip tells secrets, so don't hang around with someone who talks too much." Recall a secret or something confidential that someone shared with you about another person recently.

  - How did you feel about being told someone's private information?

  - Did you share it with anyone else—even under the guise of a prayer request?

  - What personal secret of yours can you recall sharing with someone who you now know to be a gossiper? Know that if she has told you someone else's secret, there is a good chance she is sharing yours with others!

5. Is there someone at work, church, or in your family you have

decided you would never trust with confidential information? How did this person lose his credibility with you?

6. Is there a person in your life who has probably made the decision not to trust you with confidential information? If so, how did you lose your credibility?

7. Describe the steps you are taking, or are willing to take, to establish a reputation as a person who does not engage in gossip.

Scriptures to Ponder for the Gossiping Tongue

Listening to gossip is like eating cheap candy;
do you want junk like that in your belly?
PROVERBS 26:22 MSG

A gossip goes around spreading rumors,
while a trustworthy man tries to quiet them.
PROVERBS 11:13 TLB

Don't eavesdrop on the conversation of others.
What if the gossip's about you and you'd rather not hear it?
ECCLESIASTES 7:21 MSG

When a leader listens to malicious gossip,
all the workers get infected with evil.
PROVERBS 29:12 MSG

Day 11

The Meddling Tongue

Most people are tempted at some point to interfere in the lives of others—especially when they feel they know what is best. This behavior is offensive to most other people and may cause someone to make a wrong decision simply to rebel against the unsolicited input. Further, intervention in the affairs of others may result in the loss of the relationship.

1. Begin this lesson by reading Day 11, "The Meddling Tongue," from your personal copy of *30 Days to Taming Your Tongue*. Note here at least one truth you found beneficial in your quest for a wholesome tongue.

2. Sometimes people meddle in the affairs of others under the guise of protecting them when in fact, the underlying motive is to promote their own agenda. We must always remember to respect the rights of others to make decisions for their lives. (Minors and dependent adults are exempt from this suggestion.) Describe a situation in which you stuck your nose into someone's business, only to experience a negative reaction.

3. In 1 Peter 4:15, prying into other people's affairs is given equal weight with three other sins. List them below.

   1.

   2.

   3.

4. Perhaps you're not a meddler, but often interact with those who are. Write below what your God-honoring response would be if someone were to ask you...

   • your weight:

   • your annual salary:

   • the details of a very personal surgery:

   • personal information about your pastor:

5. Your friends have come to you and asked you to deal with the extreme inquisitiveness of one of your mutual acquaintances. They have elected you to tell him to stop prying into their affairs. Rather than taking a hands-off attitude, you accept the task. What does Galatians 6:1 say about how you should approach him? In light of this Scripture, write a brief statement below regarding what you might say to him.

6. If you've decided you must intervene in the affairs of another, try these tips to increase your chance of being heard and to avoid being labeled as a "Nosey Rosey":

   • Be honest as to why you want to interfere. Ask yourself, *Is my intervention for this person's best interest, or am I attempting to promote my own agenda?*

   • Consider the history of your relationship with this person. Have you always been supportive and thus earned the right to interfere?

   • Remember that your goal is to be helpful. Therefore, refrain from using words that are judgmental, hurtful, or uncaring.

   • Don't lecture or nag. Simply state the emotional, physical, financial, relational, or spiritual impact the person's actions are having on you, others, or himself.

- Don't expect the person to agree with you right away or to quickly embrace and implement all you suggest. Give him time and space to absorb your input.

- Pledge your support to seeing the person through to the needed change.

7. List at least three conditions or situations where it would be prudent to intervene in someone's affairs. Is there someone who needs your intervention now?

1.

2.

3.

Scriptures to Ponder for the Meddling Tongue

A busybody is revealing secret counsel,
and the faithful of spirit is covering the matter.

PROVERBS 11:13 YOUNG'S

We hear that some among you are idle.
They are not busy; they are busybodies.
Such people we command and urge in the
Lord Jesus Christ to settle down.

2 THESSALONIANS 3:11-12 NIV

God is in charge of deciding human destiny.
Who do you think you are to meddle in the destiny of others?

JAMES 4:12 MSG

Like one who seizes a dog by the ears is a passer-by
who meddles in a quarrel not his own.

PROVERBS 26:17 NIV

Day 12

The Betraying Tongue

In the realm of human relationships, almost everyone will inevitably break his commitment to guard the well-being of a person he claims to love or support. Of course, the people we love have the most power to hurt us, and vice versa. Further, we expect others such as bosses, employees, pastors, and so on—based upon the usually supportive nature of the relationship—to always act in our best interest. Betrayals happen in various degrees and can have a devastating impact.

1. Begin this lesson by reading Day 12, "The Betraying Tongue," from your personal copy of *30 Days to Taming Your Tongue*. Note here at least one truth you found beneficial in your quest for a wholesome tongue.

2. Proverbs 11:13 says, "A gossip betrays a confidence, but a trustworthy man keeps a secret" (NIV). Name three people whom you believe you can trust with a secret. Indicate what your relationship is to each one.

Name   Relationship

1. _____   _____

2. _____   _____

3. _____   _____

3. What character traits or behaviors have you observed in the people above that caused them to make the list? Which of these traits do you possess?

4. According to chapter 11's discussion (page 55), a betrayer divulges information in breach of a confidence. Have you ever *deliberately* breached a confidence or engaged in an act with the hopes of negatively impacting someone?

5. Sometimes, we may not fully recognize our deep-seated anger or resentment toward another and may subconsciously sabotage her in some way. Are you willing to open your heart to the searchlight of the Word to see if this may be so? Consider God's words to the prophet Jeremiah:

The heart is deceitful above all things, and desperately wicked: who can know it? I the LORD search the heart, I try the reins, even to give every man according to his ways, and according to the fruit of his doings (Jeremiah 17:9-10 KJV).

Write a short prayer below asking God to open your eyes to any possible resentment toward another and to close the door to any subtle betrayal.

6. Read the story of Ziba's betrayal of his master, Mephibosheth, to King David, as recorded in 2 Samuel 9:1-13; 16:1-4; 19:17-29.

    • What was Ziba's motive for the betrayal?

    • What tactics did he use to effect the betrayal (2 Samuel 16:1-4)?

    • According to 2 Samuel 19:29, what did Mephibosheth lose as a result of the betrayal?

• In 2 Samuel 19:30, what was Mephibosheth's response to Ziba's disloyalty and the king's decision regarding the property division? How would you have responded had you been the king?

7. Paul warned Timothy that in the last days, people "will betray their friends" (2 Timothy 3:4). Perhaps you have never betrayed someone, but you have experienced hurtful disloyalty from someone you trusted. What was your reaction when you learned of the betrayal? What are your feelings toward that person today? If you are still harboring unforgiveness, ask God to help you to release the offender so that *you* may be free to receive His forgiveness.

8. Sometimes when people are betrayed, they blame themselves for daring to trust someone in the first place. Such a response becomes the breeding ground for cynicism. Describe the behavior of someone you have observed who is cynical because of a betrayal.

Scriptures to Ponder
for the Betraying Tongue

A gossip betrays a confidence,
but a trustworthy man keeps a secret.

PROVERBS 11:13 NIV

O LORD my God, if I have done wrong or am guilty of injustice,
if I have betrayed a friend or plundered my enemy without cause,
then let my enemies capture me. Let them trample me into the ground.
Let my honor be left in the dust.

PSALM 7:3-5

In the heat of an argument, don't betray confidences;
word is sure to get around, and no one will trust you.

PROVERBS 25:9-10 MSG

This friend of mine...betrayed me; he broke his promises.
His words are as smooth as cream, but in his heart is war.
His words are as soothing as lotion, but underneath are daggers!

PSALM 55:20-21

Day 13

The Belittling Tongue

People often belittle others to make themselves feel good or feel important, or to mask their inadequacies. Denigrating another in order to enhance one's own image is a sure sign of insecurity. Such behavior runs afoul of Paul's admonition in Ephesians 4:29 that we are to build each other up.

1. Begin this lesson by reading Day 13, "The Belittling Tongue," from your personal copy of *30 Days to Taming Your Tongue*. Note here at least one truth you found beneficial in your quest for a wholesome tongue.

2. "Death and life are in the power of the tongue: and they that love it shall eat the fruit thereof" (Proverbs 18:21 KJV). List below phrases that bring life to (build up) a person and phrases that speak death (tear down).

Life-giving phrases:
Example: "You can do it!"

- _____
- _____
- _____

Death-producing phrases:
Example: "You always mess up."

- _____
- _____
- _____

3. When you ridicule others you hurt yourself; when you build up others, you become a people magnet and a great witness for our Lord. Try these strategies for eliminating your put-down tendencies:

- If you can't say something nice, don't say anything at all.

- Don't define a person by his shortcomings; everybody has some assets. Why, even a broken clock is correct two times in a day!

- Notice things that people do right. Praise them for it.

- Ask for godly wisdom in giving constructive feedback; leave the person with hope.

- Don't make negative remarks about someone in the presence of others.

- Don't minimize anyone's pain, fears, or experience; it's their reality.

4. "Let us aim for harmony in the church and try to build each other up" (Romans 14:19). Disunity is often rampant in the church. The quest for unity starts at an individual level. Make a commitment now to call two people (leaders, volunteers, employees, and so on) from your church in the next seven days with the purpose of building them up.

5. Set a goal today of building up everyone with whom you interact. Try giving a sincere compliment, acknowledging an accomplishment, or expressing your faith in someone's ability to succeed. Make a note of at least two people you encountered and the impact your encouraging words appeared to have on each one.

6. In 1 Samuel 17:28, Eliab attempted to belittle David when he came down to the battlefield and expressed his confidence that he could subdue Goliath the giant. Write Eliab's belittling statement below.

7. Goliath belittled David because of the weapon with which he chose to fight him. Consider his denigrating words in 1 Samuel 17:43-44. David was not deterred by Goliath's or Eliab's put-downs. Write David's response (verse 45) to Goliath here.

8. Some have resorted to belittling others in an attempt to motivate them. Have you ever engaged in such behavior? Or, have you ever been a victim of negative motivation? Did it work? Explain.

Scriptures to Ponder for the Belittling Tongue

Encourage one another and build each other up,
just as in fact you are doing.
1 THESSALONIANS 5:11 NIV

Do not let any unwholesome talk come out of your mouths,
but only what is helpful for building others up according to their needs,
that it may benefit those who listen.
EPHESIANS 4:29 NIV

A wise woman builds her house;
a foolish woman tears hers down with her own hands.
PROVERBS 14:1

Day 14

The Cynical Tongue

Cynical people are angry, disappointed, resentful, and mistrustful of those they feel should be acting in their best interest. Like a rotten apple in a barrel of good ones, a cynic can negatively impact everybody he touches. Cynicism exists in every environment: in the home, on the job, in the government, in social organizations. It seems to thrive particularly well in churches where members feel their ideas and suggestions regarding the ministry are consistently ignored. They finally lose hope of ever making a difference. Resorting to cynicism becomes their coping strategy for feeling powerless to effect change. It is time to take a hard look at the ungodliness of this attitude.

1. Begin this lesson by reading Day 14, "The Cynical Tongue," from your personal copy of *30 Days to Taming Your Tongue.* Note here at least one truth you found beneficial in your quest for a wholesome tongue.

2. Read Psalm 1:1-3 and highlight it in your Bible. What do

you think it means to sit "in the seat of the scornful" (verse 1 NKJV)?

3. What three blessings are promised in Psalm 1:3 to those who resist cynicism?

   1.

   2.

   3.

4. Because cynicism is a coping mechanism for those who feel powerless to effect change in their lives, people will often make up their own reasons why the state of affairs exists, in order to deal with their hopelessness. Is there an environment in your life in which you have lost any hope of ever seeing a desired change? What rationalizations do you make to yourself (or others) as to why things will never change?

5. Cynics must remind themselves that God is in control of every situation. Therefore, the best and most godly response is to declare, "The will of the Lord be done!" God will often allow certain circumstances to persist in order to develop

character or to motivate His child to pursue a different route to his destiny.

Describe a period in your life (church, business, family, and so on) in which you responded to a situation by becoming cynical. What unmet expectations did you have? If the problem exists currently, solicit the objective input and counsel of a mature Christian. Consider re-evaluating the reasonableness of your expectations.

6. In 2 Kings 7:1, the prophet Elisha, in the midst of a famine, prophesied to the king that there would be an abundant supply of food within the next 24 hours. The king's officer responded with a cynical remark, due to the apparently hopeless situation. What did he say (verse 2) and what fate did he ultimately meet (verse 17) as a result of his cynicism? (Read 2 Kings 6:24–7:20 for the entire story.)

7. Read Romans 8:28 and write it out below. Do you embrace this truth for every aspect of your life—even for the situation in which you are tempted to be cynical?

8. If you are a leader, manager, or other person who impacts the livelihood or well-being of others, and you desire to minimize

the development of cynicism in your realm of influence, consider the strategies below:

- Keep key supervisors, team leaders, or others of influence involved in the decision-making process. People will embrace change better if they believe their preferences, suggestions, and opinions have been represented, genuinely heard, and considered.

- Keep people informed of changes in originally-agreed-upon plans or decisions—else they may feel they have been ignored or have become victims of "bait and switch" tactics. Never surprise them with an announcement of an unexpected negative decision. All surprises should be pleasant.

- Validate people's feelings by addressing their concerns with open and honest dialog. Provide good rationale as to why a course of action cannot be taken.

- Acknowledge, admit responsibility, and apologize for past mistakes and bad decisions. Explain what actions will be taken in the future to avoid further problems. People will connect with you better when you show vulnerability by apologizing rather than when you try to justify your actions.

- Where possible, confront the cynic and ask what you can do to help restore his trust.

Scriptures to Ponder
for the Cynical Tongue

*Cynics look high and low for wisdom—and never find it;
the open-minded find it right on their doorstep!*

PROVERBS 14:6 MSG

*Cast out the scoffer, and contention will leave;
yes, strife and reproach will cease.*

PROVERBS 22:10 NKJV

*Simpletons! How long will you wallow in ignorance?
Cynics! How long will you feed your cynicism?
Idiots! How long will you refuse to learn?*

PROVERBS 1:22 MSG

Day 15

The Know-It-All Tongue

While God desires for us to have many of His attributes, omniscience is not one of them. He is the only one who knows everything. Further, the Scriptures are replete with many reminders that all wisdom and knowledge come from Him. Daniel summed it up best with these powerful words: "He gives wisdom to the wise and knowledge to the discerning" (Daniel 2:21 NIV).

1. Begin this lesson by reading Day 15, "The Know-It-All Tongue," from your personal copy of *30 Days to Taming Your Tongue*. Note here at least one truth you found beneficial in your quest for a wholesome tongue.

2. What subject or area of interest are you the most knowledgeable about?

3. How did you acquire your expertise in the area above? Does the means through which you acquired your knowledge (for example, through formal education, independent study, life experience, mentorship, and so on) cause pride to rise up in you?

4. Read Proverbs 13:18 and highlight it in your Bible. What two consequences are listed for those who refuse to accept instruction?

   1.

   2.

5. Become conscious of your "know-it-all" lingo as you interact with others. Note the number of times you are tempted to use phrases such as "What you don't understand is that…"; "I know that"; "What you should do is…" Avoid these expressions whenever possible.

6. See how many times today you can ask for and listen to input from others. Be genuine in your interest. Make a note of each instance below.

7. When you attend an interactive Bible study or other meeting, try the following strategies:

- Do not correct anyone unless it is a matter of major importance.

- Refuse to become defensive or try to prove you are right if someone corrects you.

- Don't be the authority; talk less and ask more questions.

8. If you must deal with a know-it-all, remember the following:

- He'll be right most of the time, so don't directly challenge his knowledge.

- Get your facts straight or he will dismiss you as incompetent.

- Don't interrupt—a know-it-all is usually a control freak.

- Disagree wisely by simply paraphrasing his statements and asking for clarification.

- Don't be intimidated into keeping quiet—unless you are not prepared with the facts!

Scriptures to Ponder
for the Know-It-All Tongue

Wise people don't make a show of their knowledge.

PROVERBS 12:23

If you reject criticism, you only harm yourself;
but if you listen to correction, you grow in understanding.

PROVERBS 15:32

Although being a "know-it-all" makes us feel important,
what is really needed to build the church is love.
If anyone thinks he knows all the answers,
he is just showing his ignorance.
But the person who truly loves God is the one
who is open to God's knowledge.

1 CORINTHIANS 8:1-3 TLB

Pride lands you flat on your face;
humility prepares you for honors.

PROVERBS 29:23 MSG

Day 16

The Harsh Tongue

Words never die. They lodge permanently in the heart of the hearer. Because they have such long-lasting impact, it behooves us to release them with wisdom and care. Harshness emanates from our fleshly nature which, in its selfishness, fails to stop and understand the impact of our communication. Kindness, on the other hand, is produced in us by the Holy Spirit, who wants to dwell in our hearts continually and to impact our every word. Harshness at its extreme becomes verbal abuse. Unlike physical abuse which attacks the body, verbal abuse attacks a person's soul—the very core of their being.

1. Begin this lesson by reading Day 16, "The Harsh Tongue," from your personal copy of *30 Days to Taming Your Tongue*. Note here at least one truth you found beneficial in your quest for a wholesome tongue.

2. What is the harshest thing you can recall ever saying to someone?

- What motivated you to make this comment?

- What was your emotional state at the time?

- Did you apologize? What did you say when you did so? Did you rationalize your behavior or blame the victim for "making" you act this way? (If you have not apologized, write a practice script below and set a time to apologize.)

- Did you repeat this behavior at a subsequent time with the same person? If so, what do you think you can do, or what have others suggested you do, to stop this destructive pattern? If you have already gained control, what has caused you to do so?

3. People who have been victims of harsh words will often attempt to show their displeasure in some manner that is

passive–aggressive or even overtly aggressive. First Samuel 25 relates the story of a very rich but harsh man:

> The name of the man was Nabal, and the name of his wife Abigail. And she was a woman of good understanding and beautiful appearance; but the man was harsh and evil in his doings (1 Samuel 25:3 NKJV).

When David was fleeing from Saul, he sent and asked Nabal to give him food for his men. Note Nabal's harsh response and David's reaction to it. Indicate below what you think your response would have been to Nabal. Would God have approved of your actions?

4. Genesis 16 highlights a key interaction between Abram's wife Sarai and her maidservant, Hagar. At Sarai's suggestion, Hagar became pregnant by Abram. When Hagar realized what an advantage she had over her barren boss, she began to despise and dishonor her. Sarai appealed to Abram for help. "So Abram said to Sarai, 'Indeed your maid is in your hand; do to her as you please.' And when Sarai dealt harshly with her, she fled from her presence" (Genesis 16:6 NKJV).

- Is there ever a justification for being harsh to someone? Explain your answer.

• Was it right for Hagar to run away? Please elaborate.

5. Even though she provoked Sarai's harsh treatment, one cannot help but admire the fact that Hagar had the wisdom to distance herself from Sarai's abuse. In so doing, her actions set a boundary as to what she would tolerate and what she would not. Note that there was no mention of further abuse when she returned home and resumed her duties. What lesson is evident on how to respond when one has been subjected to verbal abuse?

6. Sometimes, harsh words are the result of a person's impatience with a situation he has tolerated way too long. Timely confrontation of issues is critical to avoid "blowing your top" and becoming harsh. Remember these four P's for effective confrontation:

   • *Personally:* Do it yourself; don't ask or hope that another person will deliver your message.

   • *Privately:* Honor each person's fragile ego by not criticizing her, even constructively, in the presence of another.

   • *Promptly:* Don't wait too long to address a problem; the longer the wait, the greater your frustration will be.

   • *Positively:* Express your belief in the person's ability to improve his behavior or performance. Keep the focus on the problem and avoid negative words that attack the person's character or judgment (for example, *stupid, inconsiderate,* and so on).

7. Sometimes our harshest words are directed at the ones we claim to love the most. As you read the poem below, consider whether or not you need to make amends for how you have spoken to a loved one. If so, do it today!

Harsh Words Spoken

I ran into a stranger as he passed by.
"Oh, excuse me, please" was my reply.
He said, "Please excuse me too;
I wasn't watching for you."
We were very polite, this stranger and I.
We went on our way and we said goodbye.

But at home a different story is told,
how we treat our loved ones, young and old.

Later that day, cooking the evening meal,
my son stood beside me very still.
When I turned, I nearly knocked him down.
"Move out of the way," I said with a frown.
He walked away, his little heart broken.
I didn't realize how harshly I'd spoken.

While I lay awake in bed,
God's still small voice came to me and said,
"While dealing with a stranger,
common courtesy you use,
but the children you love, you seem to abuse.
Go look on the kitchen floor,
you'll find some flowers there by the door.
Those are the flowers he brought for you.
He picked them himself; pink, yellow and blue.
He stood very quietly not to spoil the surprise,
and you never saw the tears that filled his little eyes."
By this time, I felt very small,
and now my tears began to fall.

I quietly went and knelt by his bed;
"Wake up, little one, wake up," I said.
"Are these the flowers you picked for me?"
He smiled, "I found 'em out by the tree.
I picked 'em because they're pretty like you.
I knew you'd like 'em, especially the blue."
I said, "Son, I'm very sorry for the way I acted today;
I shouldn't have yelled at you that way."
He said, "Oh, Mom, that's okay.
I love you anyway."
I said, "Son, I love you too,
and I do like the flowers, especially the blue."

AUTHOR UNKNOWN

Scriptures to Ponder
for the Harsh Tongue

A gentle answer turns away wrath,
but harsh words stir up anger.
PROVERBS 15:1

Kind words are like honey—enjoyable and healthful.
PROVERBS 16:24

Some people make cutting remarks,
but the words of the wise bring healing.
PROVERBS 12:18

Get rid of all bitterness, rage, anger, harsh words, and slander,
as well as all types of malicious behavior. Instead,
be kind to each other, tenderhearted, forgiving one another,
just as God through Christ has forgiven you.
EPHESIANS 4:31-32

Day 17

The Tactless Tongue

Tact is the ability to avoid being offensive in a negative circumstance. It is learned behavior that must be developed by experience, prayer, and submission of our tongues to the wisdom and guidance of the Holy Spirit. The extent to which one develops this skill can mean the difference between life and death—usually the death of a relationship.

1. Begin this lesson by reading Day 17, "The Tactless Tongue," from your personal copy of *30 Days to Taming Your Tongue*. Note here at least one truth you found beneficial in your quest for a wholesome tongue.

2. If you were to take a poll of the people with whom you interact the most, how do you think they would rate your tactfulness on a scale of one to ten, ten being extremely gracious and tactful? Explain.

3. Nebuchadnezzar, king of Babylon, had a troublesome dream he could not remember. He charged all of his wise men to tell him what he had dreamed as well as interpret it for him—or be put to death. The lives of Daniel and his three friends were on the line along with the other wise men. "And when Arioch, the commander of the king's guard, had gone out to put to death the wise men of Babylon, Daniel spoke to him with wisdom and tact" (Daniel 2:14 NIV).

   The killings had already started when Daniel intervened. (Read the entire second chapter of Daniel for the exciting end to the story.) Even in the midst of a stressful situation, he found a way to be tactful. Notice the question he asked in verse 15. Compare the king's response to Daniel's request for more time to interpret the dream (verse 16) to how he responded when the other wise men stalled for time (verses 8-9). Could it be that tactfulness will bring us favor when we need it? Also, compare Daniel's skill at being tactful in the previous situation he was in (discussed on pages 70–71 of *30 Days to Taming Your Tongue*).

4. Read Judges 8:1-3. Why were the Ephraimites upset with Gideon? What diplomatic words did he say to them that calmed them and averted an intertribal war?

5. How would you respond if someone greeted you at a party

with this tactless remark: "That's a nice outfit. It was really the rage during its fashion season"?

6. Recall a tactless but truthful remark you made to someone. How did he respond? What amends, if any, did you make once you realized you had put your foot in your mouth?

7. Elaborate on the principle of "honesty is the best policy." Explain an instance in which it may not be.

8. If you have a tendency to be tactless, follow the steps below to developing more diplomacy:

   • Always follow the Golden Rule: "In everything, do to others what you would have them do to you, for this sums up the Law and the Prophets" (Matthew 7:12 NIV). Pretend you are the recipient of the statement that you are about to make. Ask yourself, *How would I feel if someone said this to me?*

   • Make every attempt to balance the negatives with positives. ("What Sharon lacks in experience is offset by her enthusiasm.")

- Play it safe. Assume that *everybody* is supersensitive and interact accordingly.

- When asked a no-win question such as, "Does this make me look fat?" turn the question back to the inquirer with a remark like, "More important, how does it make *you* feel? Don't turn your power of choice over to me." Or, if you are really courageous, you may respond (at your own risk), "I've seen you in outfits that may be a bit more flattering..." Pray for words that don't hurt but that don't lie!

*Scriptures to Ponder
for the Tactless Tongue*

*From a wise mind comes careful
and persuasive speech.*
PROVERBS 16:23 TLB

*A word fitly spoken is like apples of
gold in pictures of silver.*
PROVERBS 25:11 KJV

*When she speaks, her words are wise,
and kindness is the rule when she gives instructions.*
PROVERBS 31:26

*Wise speech is rarer and more valuable
than gold and rubies.*
PROVERBS 20:15

Day 18

The Intimidating Tongue

Intimidators are bullies. They major in making others feel inadequate, unworthy, ashamed, fearful—any emotion that will allow them to maintain their position of dominance. Most intimidators fit the description of the person described in Psalm 10:7, whose "mouth is full of curses and lies and threats; trouble and evil are under his tongue" (NIV). While intimidators often get their way, they are not the towers of strength they pretend to be. At the base of their behavior is a bundle of fear. Healing will only come when they acknowledge their fears and seek deliverance through counseling and the power of the Holy Spirit.

1. Begin this lesson by reading Day 18, "The Intimidating Tongue," from your personal copy of *30 Days to Taming Your Tongue*. Note here at least one truth you found beneficial in your quest for a wholesome tongue.

2. When Nehemiah was rebuilding the walls of Jerusalem, a certain group of men tried to intimidate him into quitting.

Read Nehemiah 6:1-17. List below at least one tactic that they used to deter the work.

- What was Nehemiah's response to them?

- What example did Nehemiah set for us in his prayer to God (verse 14) regarding his intimidators?

3. While it is not common for women to be intimidators, Jezebel intimidated one of the most powerful prophets in the Bible. Read the story in 1 Kings 18:19-40; 19:1-4.

- What prophet did she view as her nemesis, and what did he do to arouse her anger?

- What threats did she make in response to his offense (1 Kings 19:2)?

• How did he respond to her threats (1 Kings 19:3-4)?

4. Read Acts 4:13-31. How did Peter and John respond to the chief priests and elders' threats to stop preaching the gospel? Has someone ever tried to threaten or intimidate you and keep you from doing God's will? Note that even the threat of alienation from group fellowship is enough to deter some people. Describe the situation and how you came out of it.

5. Have you ever tried to control someone's behavior by making a subtle threat? What were the results? What do you think the outcome would have been if you had not introduced the element of fear? Why did you think your threat was more powerful than prayer?

6. Have you observed that most intimidators do not have close relationships with others? They seem to be totally oblivious to the fact that the average person has no desire to be disrespected, disparaged, or disregarded. Please comment on this observation.

7. When John the Baptist was baptizing people in the wilderness, various groups came to be baptized. They had many questions about how they should behave after baptism. From among these groups, "the soldiers asked him, saying, 'And what shall we do?' So he said to them, 'Do not intimidate anyone or accuse falsely, and be content with your wages'" (Luke 3:14 NKJV). In your opinion, is it ever appropriate for those who are to uphold the law to intimidate others? Explain.

8. Intimidation runs rampant in many marriages. Review the list of behaviors below and note how many of them describe your actions or that of your spouse:

    • making demeaning remarks

    • threatening (divorce, suicide, murder, taking the kids, and so on)

    • having a demanding attitude (no appreciation or common courtesies)

    • running guilt trips

    • invalidating the feelings, opinions, and thoughts of the spouse

9. As an intimidator, what specific plans have you made for getting help?

10. If you are the victim of an intimidator (at home, work, or church), write out the impact his behavior has had upon you physically and emotionally. How long do you plan to tolerate this situation? Whom have you solicited for needed emotional support?

Scriptures to Ponder for the Intimidating Tongue

Don't be intimidated by your enemies.
This will be a sign to them that they are going to be destroyed,
but that you are going to be saved, even by God himself.

PHILIPPIANS 1:28

My enemies lay traps for me; they make plans to ruin me.
They think up treacherous deeds all day long. But I am deaf to all their
threats. I am silent before them as one who cannot speak.
I choose to hear nothing, and I make no reply. For I am waiting for you,
O LORD. You must answer for me, O LORD my God.

PSALM 38:12-15

O Lord, hear their threats,
and give your servants great boldness.

ACTS 4:29

Day 19

The Rude Tongue

According to American philosopher Eric Hoffer, "Rudeness is the weak man's imitation of strength, and luxuriates in the absence of self-respect." Rudeness is on the rise in our society and needs to be addressed in our personal lives since change begins on an individual level. In the final analysis, rudeness stems from a heart of selfishness and the blatant disregard of the rights of others.

1. Begin this lesson by reading Day 19, "The Rude Tongue," from your personal copy of *30 Days to Taming Your Tongue*. Note here at least one truth you found beneficial in your quest for a wholesome tongue.

2. Has anyone ever accused you of being rude?_____ If so, what did you do to merit their assessment? How would you have responded if someone had done the same to you?

3. To whom (individual or group) are you most likely to be rude or unkind? Why?

4. List three acts of rudeness discussed on page 82 of *30 Days to Taming Your Tongue.*

   1.

   2.

   3.

   Do you have a habit of engaging in these acts?

5. Besides the ones listed above, consider the following additional acts of rudeness and inconsiderateness set forth below. Circle each one you have been guilty of committing in the last year. See how many rude or inconsiderate acts you can add to the list.

   • using foul language in public

   • making fun of someone's appearance or physical handicap

   • staring

- refusing to say hello when your customer approaches the register

- piling your plate high with food at a party when others are waiting to serve themselves

- cutting into the line at the bank, supermarket, or other public places

- pointing out someone's shortcoming or inadequacy

- name-calling

- calling someone fat

- being condescending

- changing the subject while someone is talking

- starting a side conversation with another person while socializing with a group

- slurping, smacking, sucking your teeth, and making other annoying noises

- failing to speak to people in the hallways at work or church

- not saying "good morning" or "good evening" to family members

- snapping your fingers to get a food server's attention

- yawning without covering your mouth

- not saying "please" when making a request of anyone

- not saying "excuse me" when you inconvenience someone

- putting callers on hold without asking for permission to do so

- transferring a caller to another extension without advance warning

- reaching across someone to pick up something

- switching the channel on the TV without acknowledging the desires of other viewers in the room

- yelling at your kids in public (regular discipline at home should negate this need)

- popping chewing gum

- other: _____

6. "When the poor speak, they have to beg politely, but when the rich answer, they are rude" (Proverbs 18:23 GNT).

- Has this been your experience with the affluent or powerful people with whom you have interacted? Explain.

- Have you ever been rude to someone less fortunate than you? Why?

7. People act in a rude manner either because they think it is okay or they feel they can get away with it. While most of us will feel righteous indignation at being subjected to rude acts, we must practice confronting in God-honoring ways. Otherwise, our silence may only reinforce the behavior. The next

time someone is rude to you in a public place, try the *shame game* by pointing out the rude behavior. Most people don't want others to think badly of them, so this may work.

(Caution! In other one-on-one situations, please use wisdom in confronting rudeness. If the person looks unsavory or hostile, just grin and bear it. Better to be safe than sorry!)

Scriptures to Ponder
for the Rude Tongue

Answering before listening is both stupid and rude.
PROVERBS 18:13 MSG

If you're dumb enough to call attention to yourself
by offending people and making rude gestures,
don't be surprised if someone bloodies your nose.
Churned milk turns into butter;
riled emotions turn into fist fights. Speak out for justice.
PROVERBS 30:32-33 MSG

Love is patient and kind. Love is not jealous or boastful or
proud or rude. Love does not demand its own way. Love is not
irritable, and it keeps no record of when it has been wronged.
1 CORINTHIANS 13:4-5

There will be a highway called the Holy Road.
No one rude or rebellious is permitted on this road.
It's for God's people exclusively.
ISAIAH 35:8 MSG

Day 20

The Judgmental Tongue

There is a difference between making judgments and being judgmental. We all must make practical judgments on a daily basis regarding what is best for our lives and those for whom we are responsible. On a spiritual level, we must discern and judge what we feel is from the Holy Spirit and what is not. We become judgmental when we conclude that other people are wrong, unspiritual, or inferior in some manner because they do not embrace the judgments we would make for ourselves. Being judgmental is contrary to the will of God.

1. Begin this lesson by reading Day 20, "The Judgmental Tongue," from your personal copy of *30 Days to Taming Your Tongue*. Note here at least one truth you found beneficial in your quest for a wholesome tongue.

2. Based upon our upbringing, socialization, and life experiences, we all have opinions about how certain things should be and how people should look or behave. In

John 7:24, Jesus cautioned the church to "stop judging by mere appearances, and make a right judgment" (NIV).

Indicate below the areas where you already have a mindset that negatively prejudges a person or group by surface appearance. Here is a list to get you started. Circle all that apply to you and complete the list by adding your other prejudices. As you review each one, ask yourself, *How does this person or group impact the quality of my personal life? Why does their existence or life choice matter so much to me? Am I harboring a deep-seated fear that I, or someone I love, will become like them? What is at the base of my negative feelings?*

- certain ethnic groups

- right-wing or left-wing politicians

- gay people

- obese people

- loud people

- people with tattoos

- people with brightly colored hair

- women who dress immodestly

- teenagers

- _____

- _____

- _____

- _____

- _____

- _____

3. To judge properly is to form an opinion or draw a conclusion based upon reliable information and other objective evidence. People will often judge based upon limited data, hearsay, or unsubstantiated information. This is totally contrary to the Scriptures. "Does our law judge a man before it hears him and knows what he is doing?" (John 7:51 NKJV).

   Have you ever made a judgment about someone, only to discover you were wrong in your assessment because you were not aware of all of the facts? Explain what happened and how you dealt with the newfound truth.

4. Read 1 Corinthians 5:9-13. What does Paul say about which groups we are to judge and which ones we are to leave to God?

5. Who has been the most judgmental person in your life? What does he or she do to show disapproval of your choices? How has this impacted how you judge others?

6. People who are judgmental are not usually surrounded by lots of adoring friends and family members. Is there someone you deliberately avoid because of his judgmental personality?

Why haven't you discussed this failing with him, as recommended in Galatians 6:1?

7. Judgmental people tend to be dogmatic in stating their views. They act as if their opinion is the final authority; they evaluate people's behavior and place a permanent label on them. They are the moral cops of the universe. Note below at least three judgmental beliefs that are etched in your mind (*example:* "Obese people are lazy").

- _____

- _____

- _____

Ask the Holy Spirit to take away all judgmental thinking and to give you a heart of love and acceptance. Know that acceptance of a *person* does not mean acceptance of his *sin*.

Scriptures to Ponder for the Judgmental Tongue

Stop judging others, and you will not be judged.
For others will treat you as you treat them.
Whatever measure you use in judging others,
it will be used to measure how you are judged.
MATTHEW 7:1-2

You are inexcusable, O man, whoever you are who judge,
for in whatever you judge another you condemn yourself;
for you who judge practice the same things.
ROMANS 2:1 NKJV

God alone, who made the law, can rightly judge among us.
He alone has the power to save or to destroy.
So what right do you have to condemn your neighbor.
JAMES 4:12

Valid criticism is as treasured by the one who heeds it
as jewelry made from finest gold.
PROVERBS 25:12

Don't jump to conclusions—there may be a perfectly
good explanation for what you just saw.
PROVERBS 25:8 MSG

Day 21

The Self-Absorbed Tongue

Everyone needs to know he matters to somebody. Everybody also needs an opportunity to express his concerns, challenges, desires, and hopes with a caring listener. The problem arises when one person esteems his issues above those of all others. He is totally preoccupied with himself. He becomes a relational challenge when others realize that their interaction with him is one-sided, with no mutual sharing of needs or ideas.

1. Begin this lesson by reading Day 21, "The Self-Absorbed Tongue," from your personal copy of *30 Days to Taming Your Tongue*. Note here at least one truth you found beneficial in your quest for a wholesome tongue.

2. If you are self-absorbed, know that it is learned behavior. Somebody allowed you to become the center of attention. Perhaps you were the only child, the youngest, or the most frail, or have some other distinction that caused you to receive most of the focus in your environment as a

child. Also know that in any relationships, there has to be mutual sharing and caring for it to work God's way.

Observe your conversations today and notice whether you subtly (or deliberately) manipulate the discussions to focus on your issues. Note how often you say "I." Write your observations here at the end of the day.

3. Read Esther 5:1-12. Name five things that Haman boasted about to his family and friends. Search the entire chapter to see if he ever expressed an interest in *their* issues.

   1.

   2.

   3.

   4.

   5.

4. Narcissus was a character in Greek mythology who was always looking at his own reflection. He was the most important thing in his world. Narcissistic, self-absorbed people think the world exists to serve them. When people cater to them, it only reinforces their mind-set. If there is a self-absorbed person in your life whom you care about and wish to help, then you must accept the challenge of getting her to embrace

a new paradigm—acknowledging there are other people on planet earth with a life to *share*. Here are some strategies for starters:

- Have her agree to let you help her with this problem.

- Do not indulge her selfishness; do not let her "hog" your conversations.

- Insist that she listen and give you feedback on other topics of interest.

- Whenever she tries to refocus the discussion on herself, just get quiet and do not respond.

- Don't give up; you're preparing her for godly relationships.

5. Write out a prayer asking God to deliver you from being self-absorbed and to help you become genuinely interested in others.

Scriptures to Ponder for the Self-Absorbed Tongue

Don't think only about your own affairs,
but be interested in others too, and what they are doing.
PHILIPPIANS 2:4

Mark this: There will be terrible times in the last days.
People will be lovers of themselves…having a form of godliness
but denying its power. Have nothing to do with them.
2 TIMOTHY 3:1,5 NIV

Share each other's troubles and problems,
and in this way obey the law of Christ.
GALATIANS 6:2

A man who isolates himself seeks his own desire;
he rages against all wise judgment.
PROVERBS 18:1 NKJV

Day 22

The Cursing Tongue

Obscenities, vulgarity, cursing, and using profanity all fall into the same category of behavior that emanates from conditions of the heart. Engaged in by Christians and non-Christians alike, this crude use of the tongue is an affront to our heavenly Father. Notwithstanding, such use of the tongue is not usually premeditated but results from a response to sudden pain, anger, hurt, or frustration. It is learned behavior that must be rooted out and brought under submission to the Holy Spirit.

1. Begin this lesson by reading Day 22, "The Cursing Tongue," from your personal copy of *30 Days to Taming Your Tongue*. Note here at least one truth you found beneficial in your quest for a wholesome tongue.

2. List two reasons given on page 94 of *30 Days to Taming Your Tongue* as to why people use profanity.

    1.

    2.

3. What does Luke 6:45 say about the real source of all evil speaking? Write the Scripture verse out here and meditate on it a few minutes before proceeding to the next question.

4. Read Mark 14:66-72. Discuss below what Peter's emotional state must have been (fearful, angry, and so on) for him to resort to cursing.

5. Woodrow Wilson's father, Dr. Joseph R. Wilson, was a godly and distinguished Presbyterian minister in the South. The story has it that he was once in the company of men who were having a heated discussion. In the midst of it, one let out a profane expletive. Then, seeing Dr. Wilson there, he offered an apology, saying, "Sir, I had forgotten that you were present. Please pardon me." Dr. Wilson's reply was, "It is not to me that you owe your apology but to God." *

   Do people honor you in this way when they inadvertently use profanity in your presence? Or, are you the one making the apology for such base language? Explain.

---

* Paul Lee Tan. *Encyclopedia of 7000 Illustrations* (Garland, TX: Bible Communications, 1996).

6. If profanity just seems to "slip" from your lips, write out a prayer decreeing your deliverance. Include Psalm 39:1 as part of your declaration of freedom.

Scriptures to Ponder for the Cursing Tongue

No one can tame the tongue. It is an uncontrollable evil,
full of deadly poison. Sometimes it praises our Lord and Father,
and sometimes it breaks out into curses against those who have been
made in the image of God. And so blessing and cursing come pouring
out of the same mouth. Surely, my brothers and sisters, this is not right!
JAMES 3:8-10

Nor is it fitting for you to use language which is obscene,
profane, or vulgar. Rather you should give thanks to God.
You may be sure that no one who is immoral, indecent,
or greedy (for greed is a form of idolatry) will ever receive a
share in the Kingdom of Christ and of God.
EPHESIANS 5:4-5 GNT

You shall not swear by My name falsely,
nor shall you profane the name of your God: I am the LORD.
LEVITICUS 19:12 NKJV

Guard your tongue from profanity,
and no more lying through your teeth.
PSALM 34:13 MSG

Day 23

The Complaining Tongue

No matter how well everything else is going, most people can find something to express their disapproval, displeasure, or dissatisfaction about—be it the weather, the traffic, the long lines, the cold food, the slow service, the pastor, the church, the boss, the workload, the low pay, the short vacation, inadequate benefits, bad drivers, rising prices…the list is endless. It is the nature of man to complain.

Prior to going on a recent trip to Hawaii, I decided to go on a "complaining fast." During the trip, I caught and stopped myself from complaining out loud about the heavy traffic going to the airport, the slow security-screening process, the unavailability of hot meals on the plane, the five-hour duration of the flight from Los Angeles to Maui, the amount of money we were spending on tips…and on and on it went. And the trip was just starting!

I finally just said "Stop!" to my thoughts and began to focus on the things that were of a good report. I decided to be grateful that we had the resources to afford such a wonderful trip, that we were attending a very popular wealth-building conference with five delightful couples from our church, that I was now pain-free and completely off of debilitating medications following brain surgery only ten weeks prior, and finally, that my wonderful husband and I were celebrating our twenty-eighth wedding anniversary. To boot, I had been asked to speak at the next year's conference. The invitation, which I had secretly desired, was an answer to prayer and had come only days before the trip.

It is interesting to note that the list of things we can be grateful for is always a lot longer than our complaint list when we make a conscious effort to train our minds to follow the apostle Paul's admonition in Philippians 4:8:

> Whatever things are true, whatever things are noble,
> whatever things are just, whatever things are pure,
> whatever things are lovely, whatever things are of
> good report, if there is any virtue and if there is any-
> thing praiseworthy—meditate on these things.

1. Begin this lesson by reading Day 23, "The Complaining Tongue," from your personal copy of *30 Days to Taming Your Tongue*. Note here at least one truth you found beneficial in your quest for a wholesome tongue.

2. Complaining is by far the most common negative use of the tongue. It can be contagious if we are not on guard against it. All it takes is one chronic complainer to change the entire atmosphere. Sometimes we may not personally have a problem with a particular situation—however, to avoid hurting the complainer's feelings, or to make her feel that we are relating to her, we may chime in and join the grumbling as if we too are negatively impacted by the circumstances.

   For the next 24 hours, listen to the people around you

and make note of the various types of complaints you hear. What do you find that people complained about the most?

3. When others complain to you, try countering their negativity by first agreeing with the *reality* of their complaint *(if you do indeed agree)* and then putting a positive light on it. Practice *being* the light in a dark world. Here are some examples of how to do it:

    -   "Yes, the service is a little slow, but that just gives us more time to interact with each other."

    -   "The benefits could be better, but they sure beat having none at all."

    -   "The weather is indeed awful, but I'm just grateful to have a nice warm place called home, where I can take refuge from it."

    -   Make no comment at all. Just smile and look straight ahead! The other person(s) will get the point that you do not wish to engage the complaint.

    This approach to dealing with complainers prevents you from being sucked into an everpresent vacuum and allows you to begin to model the joy the Holy Spirit produces in those who have submitted their lives to Him. "The fruit of the Spirit is love, joy..." (Galatians 5:22 KJV).

4. Recall the last time you insincerely agreed with someone's complaint simply to go along. Write below what you could

have said instead that would have gracefully countered the complaint.

5. Now, let's shift the focus from others and put the spotlight on you. Make a commitment to refrain from expressing your displeasure with any situation for a designated period of time—at least three to seven days. Keep a pad and pencil handy, and make note of each incident in which you were tempted to complain.

6. What is the one thing you are tempted to complain about the most?

   • To whom do you complain?_____Does this person have the power to solve the problem?

   • Are you refusing to take responsibility or initiative for changing the problematic situation? Explain your answer.

7. Read Romans 8:28 in your favorite version of the Bible. Write it out below in the form of a personal proclamation by substituting "I" for "we," and so on. Repeat it throughout the day as an antidote to your temptation to complain.

8. In 1 Corinthians 10:10-11, Paul reminded the church of how God dealt with the complaining Israelites during their time in the wilderness:

> Don't grumble as some of them did, for that is why God sent his angel of death to destroy them. All these events happened to them as examples for us. They were written down to warn us, who live at the time when this age is drawing to a close.

Why do you think God gets so upset when we murmur and complain?

9. Make a pact with a friend or a group to monitor each other's tendency to complain. Mutually agree upon an acceptable "fine" for each "violation." For example, each complaint could be assessed a 5-point penalty; when the penalties reach a certain limit (say 20 points), the violator would be required to pay a set amount into a "cash kitty." At the end of the monitoring period, the accumulated funds could be donated to a charity. And hopefully, each person would have made a significant change in his grumbling habit.

10. Most complainers could improve their situations if they would simply take personal responsibility for their plight rather than polluting the environment with their constant belly-aching. The five Israelite sisters highlighted in this chapter took the

initiative to get those in charge to correct what they felt was an unfair policy for allocating rights to property in the Promised Land. They knew that complaining to the multitude would be futile. Instead, they operated in unity and wisdom and petitioned Moses and the elders to give them their deceased father's portion of the land. Their efforts paid off, and they were granted their request.

As you review and consider the nature of your complaints, you may find it helpful to distinguish between those that are *useful* and those that are *useless*. The *useful* category includes situations that are within your circle of influence—that is, you can impact them directly or have access to someone who can. The *useless* category includes situations that are simply time-wasters. For example, you cannot do anything about traffic, the weather, long lines, and most of the rest of life's annoying realities. Your best bet is going to be to manage your life and your time in such a way that you are only minimally impacted by negative circumstances. Otherwise, know that there will always be something you'd like to see improved. Change it—or zip your lips!

Scriptures to Ponder
for the Complaining Tongue

Do all things without murmurings and disputings.
PHILIPPIANS 2:14 KJV

Giving thanks is a sacrifice that truly honors me.
If you keep to my path, I will reveal to you the salvation of God.
PSALM 50:23

Don't grumble against each other, brothers, or you will be judged.
The Judge is standing at the door!
JAMES 5:9 NIV

They knew God, but they wouldn't worship him as God or even give
him thanks. And they began to think up foolish ideas of what God was
like. The result was that their minds became dark and confused.
ROMANS 1:21

LORD, accept my grateful thanks and teach me your laws.
PSALM 119:108

I cry aloud with my voice to the LORD; I make supplication with
my voice to the LORD. I pour out my complaint before Him;
I declare my trouble before Him.
PSALM 142:1-2 NASB

Day 24

The Retaliating Tongue

According to English philosopher Francis Bacon, "A man that studies revenge keeps his own wounds green, which otherwise would heal and do well." Retaliation makes us feel that justice has been satisfied when we have been wronged.

1. Begin this lesson by reading Day 24, "The Retaliating Tongue," from your personal copy of *30 Days to Taming Your Tongue*. Note here at least one truth you found beneficial in your quest for a wholesome tongue.

2. Read Matthew 5:44. What are the four things Jesus said we must do for an enemy?

    1.

    2.

    3.

    4.

• Have you had the opportunity to do this for someone?

• Which of the four actions did you find the most problematic? Why?

3. In a recent incident in which someone wronged you, recall how you shared the transgression with others and how you felt relating the story. Did you get some satisfaction by having them learn of the person's villainous behavior? Please explain.

• Were you tempted to retaliate in any manner?

• What exactly did you desire to do? What kept you from doing so?

4. According to Proverbs 24:17-18, how are we to respond when we hear that misfortune has come to our enemies?

5. Read Genesis 50:15-22 for the final account of how Joseph "repaid" his brothers for selling him into Egyptian slavery. (The epic story of his 93 years in Egypt is found in chapters 39–50.) Write out below his response (verses 19-20) to their anxiety about being punished for their in evil deed.

6. Jesus Christ is our ultimate example of how to respond to suffering at the hands of others. What is his model as explained in 1 Peter 2:23?

7. Write out the statement from "Today's Affirmation" (page 104) and meditate on it throughout the day.

Scriptures to Ponder for the Retaliating Tongue

Don't repay evil for evil. Don't retaliate when people say unkind things about you. Instead, pay them back with a blessing. That is what God wants you to do, and he will bless you for it.

1 PETER 3:9

O LORD, the God to whom vengeance belongs,
O God of vengeance, let your glorious justice be seen!

PSALM 94:1

When they hurled their insults at him, he did not retaliate;
when he suffered, he made no threats.
Instead, he entrusted himself to him who judges justly.

1 PETER 2:23 NIV

Do not repay anyone evil for evil. Be careful to do what is right in the eyes of everybody. If it is possible, as far as it depends on you, live at peace with everyone. Do not take revenge, my friends, but leave room for God's wrath, for it is written: "It is mine to avenge; I will repay," says the Lord. On the contrary: "If your enemy is hungry, feed him; if he is thirsty, give him something to drink. In doing this, you will heap burning coals on his head."
Do not be overcome by evil, but overcome evil with good.

ROMANS 12:17-21 NIV

Day 25

The Accusing Tongue

The Bible is replete with stories and instances of false accusations being made against godly people. Such charges can derail a career, disrupt unity, and wreak havoc in a person's life. Of course, Satan is the ultimate "accuser of our brothers, who accuses them before God day and night" (Revelations 12:10 NIV). Notwithstanding, God is faithful to His children and has promised,

> No weapon turned against you will succeed. And everyone who tells lies in court will be brought to justice. These benefits are enjoyed by the servants of the LORD; their vindication will come from me. I, the LORD, have spoken (Isaiah 54:17).

1. Begin this lesson by reading Day 25, "The Accusing Tongue," from your personal copy of *30 Days to Taming Your Tongue*. Note here at least one truth you found beneficial in your quest for a wholesome tongue.

2. Read Job 22:6-11. List three failings that Job's friend Eliphaz accused him of to explain why Job was suffering. Was there an element of truth to any of his accusations?

   1.

   2.

   3.

3. In his letter, Paul instructed Titus to teach the older women to "be in behaviour as becometh holiness, not false accusers" (Titus 2:3 KJV). Have you ever made an accusation against someone, only to discover you were wrong? What did you do next? Were your actions such as "becometh holiness" (are suitable to holiness)? Explain.

4. We must always seek first to understand before making an accusation or drawing a conclusion about a person's actions. Even though God knew that Adam had eaten the forbidden fruit, He asked him three questions before banishing him from the Garden of Eden (Genesis 3:9-11). List them below. Why do you think He waited for Adam's explanation?

   1.

   2.

   3.

5. Read Daniel 6:1-23. Why did Daniel's co-workers wish to discredit him?

   • What two reasons are given (verse 4) as to why they could not make an accusation against him relative to his work habits or the quality of his work?

     1.

     2.

   • If someone wanted to accuse you of incompetence or wrongdoing in the area of your work or profession, would he have to look very far to do so? Explain.

6. Write out a prayer asking God to help you not to be a false accuser but to seek first to understand and be diligent in gathering the facts.

Scriptures to Ponder for the Accusing Tongue

Don't make accusations against someone who hasn't wronged you.

PROVERBS 3:30

Accuse not a servant unto his master, lest he curse thee, and thou be found guilty.

PROVERBS 30:10 KJV

He defends the helpless and saves them from those who accuse them.

PSALM 109:31 NCV

The Sovereign LORD himself defends me—who, then, can prove me guilty? All my accusers will disappear; they will vanish like moth-eaten cloth.

ISAIAH 50:9 GNT

Day 26

The Discouraging Tongue

Cheering fans provide a home-court advantage in sports contests. Words of encouragement can make winners out of people who maybe have thought they were failures. Everybody needs affirmation and validation at some point in their lives. Woe unto us when we have the power to speak words of motivation and hope—but choose rather to destroy a person's confidence and dreams with discouraging words.

1. Begin this lesson by reading Day 26, "The Discouraging Tongue," from your personal copy of *30 Days to Taming Your Tongue*. Note here at least one truth you found beneficial in your quest for a wholesome tongue.

2. In recounting how he gave hope during his pre-suffering days to all those with whom he dealt, Job said,

   They longed for me to speak as they longed for rain.
   They waited eagerly, for my words were as refreshing

as the spring rain. When they were discouraged, I
smiled at them. My look of approval was precious to
them (Job 29:23-25).

Are your words as refreshing as the rain, or are they more
like a wet blanket that smothers the hopes of others? Do you
make it a habit to give an approving smile to those who are
pursuing a certain goal? Explain.

3. In Joshua 1:9, Moses officially transferred to Joshua the
    responsibility for leading the Israelites into the Promised
    Land. Write below his words of encouragement set forth
    in this verse. Call up a friend or someone who needs to be
    encouraged and share this verse with them today.

4. What person has been your biggest cheerleader? Describe how
    she or he has impacted your life.

5. Have you ever *abandoned* a dream or course of action because
    of someone's discouraging words, and later regretted your
    decision to do so? Explain.

6. Have you ever pursued and accomplished a goal *despite* someone's discouraging words? Explain. What did you learn from this experience that you can share with others?

7. Go to your local variety store and pick up a box of blank greeting cards. Target at least one person per month and send him or her a brief handwritten note of encouragement. Be particularly mindful of those who are going to school, looking for a job, raising small children, recently divorced, caring for an elderly parent, or have lost a loved one. Consider including a small monetary gift or other token of appreciation.

   Note here the name of the person to whom you will send this month's card: _____

8. Consider the following additional ways to encourage others on a daily basis:

   • Take authority over your own negativity so it does not impact others.

   • Listen to the plans of others with genuine interest.

   • Share faith-building Scripture verses with them.

   • Agree in prayer with them for their success.

   • Express your confidence in their abilities.

   • Give sincere and specific compliments.

   • Reiterate your love and support.

Scriptures to Ponder
for the Discouraging Tongue

Worry weighs a person down;
an encouraging word cheers a person up.
PROVERBS 12:25

Brothers and sisters, we urge you to warn those who are lazy.
Encourage those who are timid.
Take tender care of those who are weak.
Be patient with everyone.
1 THESSALONIANS 5:14

Judas and Silas, who themselves were prophets,
said much to encourage and strengthen the brothers.
ACTS 15:32 NIV

Day 27

The Doubting Tongue

Doubt is an insidious and persistent enemy of our faith. It is perhaps Satan's most effective weapon. No matter what we do, it always manages to find a place in the deep corners of our minds—even if only for a fleeting second. Some have learned to conquer it by forging ahead in spite of its presence and standing on the promises of God. Others heed it and miss their destiny.

1. Begin this lesson by reading Day 27, "The Doubting Tongue," from your personal copy of *30 Days to Taming Your Tongue*. Note here at least one truth you found beneficial in your quest for a wholesome tongue.

2. According to Genesis 3:1, Satan's first four recorded words in the Bible were "Yea, hath God said...?" (KJV). He has attempted to cast doubt on God's words ever since. Recall the last time he tried to bring unbelief into your life. What were the circumstances, and how did you fare under his attack?

3. According to 1 John 5:10, "Anyone who does not believe God has made him out to be a _____ " (NIV).

4. What has been the biggest hurdle you have overcome in unbelief in a particular area (for example, flying, tithing, and so on)? Summarize below what you did to achieve your victory.

5. "All things, whatsoever ye shall ask in prayer, believing, ye shall receive" (Matthew 21:22 KJV). What need are you having difficulty putting into the "whatsoever" category? Why? Could it be that you are exalting the problem above the power of God?

6. Many times godly people have doubts but have learned how to run to God for assurance and strength. Read the story of King Jehoshaphat in 2 Chronicles 20. What was his first reaction (verse 3) when he learned that three strong armies were coming against him and his people?

• What two things did he do next? Do you regularly employ these strategies?

1.

2.

• Write out the portions of his prayer as recorded in 2 Chronicles 20:6,12. Consider writing these on a separate sheet also for reinforcement of your faith in times of crises.

7. List the things you do on a regular basis to keep doubts at bay.

Scriptures to Ponder for the Doubting Tongue

Without faith it is impossible to please him:
for he that cometh to God must believe that he is,
and that he is a rewarder of them that diligently seek him.
HEBREWS 11:6 KJV

Behold, I am the LORD, the God of all flesh:
is there any thing too hard for me?
JEREMIAH 32:27 KJV

Now to Him who is able to do exceedingly abundantly
above all that we ask or think, according to the power
that works in us, to Him be glory in the church by
Christ Jesus to all generations, forever and ever. Amen.
EPHESIANS 3:20-21 NKJV

Let him ask in faith, with no doubting, for he who doubts
is like a wave of the sea driven and tossed by the wind.
For let not that man suppose that he will receive anything from the
Lord; he is a double-minded man, unstable in all his ways.
JAMES 1:6-8 NKJV

Day 28

The Loquacious Tongue

A person of few words usually commands more attention when he speaks. Perhaps this is so because others assume his words have been chosen carefully after much thought and deliberation, unlike the words of those who constantly spill them out from an apparently unlimited supply source.

1. Begin this lesson by reading Day 28, "The Loquacious Tongue," from your personal copy of *30 Days to Taming Your Tongue*. Note here at least one truth you found beneficial in your quest for a wholesome tongue.

2. According to 1 Peter 3:4, women should adorn themselves with "a meek and quiet spirit, which is in the sight of God of great price" (KJV). Comment on why a quiet spirit is so valuable. Could it be because it is rare?

3. Excessive talking can have a negative impact on your career and social standing. For sure, it can have a detrimental spiritual impact, according to Proverbs 10:19. By exercising a little objectivity, you can judge for yourself whether you talk too much. Here are a few questions to consider:

- Would the people in your circle of interaction classify you as a talker or a listener?

- In conversations with others, do you talk for more than one to two minutes at a time?

- Do you notice signs of loss of interest in what you are saying (people wandering off, eyes darting to the other side of the room, tapping fingers on the table or desk, and so on)?

- Are you likely to provide lots of details in your stories?

- Do you forget to draw others into your conversation and assume they like hearing you talk?

If you answered yes to at least three of these questions, you might consider developing a new strategy for your interactions.

4. Write out "Today's Affirmation" from the next page. Repeat this personal proclamation to yourself throughout the day.

Scriptures to Ponder for the Loquacious Tongue

Study to be quiet...
1 THESSALONIANS 4:11 KJV

When words are many, sin is not absent,
but he who holds his tongue is wise.
PROVERBS 10:19 NIV

The man of few words and settled mind is wise; therefore,
even a fool is thought to be wise when he is silent.
It pays him to keep his mouth shut.
PROVERBS 17:27 TLB

Don't make rash promises to God, for he is in heaven,
and you are only here on earth. So let your words be few.
ECCLESIASTES 5:2

Today's Affirmation

When my words are many, sin is not absent,
but when I hold my tongue, I am wise.
FROM PROVERBS 10:19 NIV

The Indiscreet Tongue

Discretion in speech is a key indicator of spiritual and emotional maturity. Saying only what is appropriate and necessary in a particular situation reflects a person's wisdom in restraining his tongue.

1. Begin this lesson by reading Day 29, "The Indiscreet Tongue," from your personal copy of *30 Days to Taming Your Tongue*. Note here at least one truth you found beneficial in your quest for a wholesome tongue.

2. "Never make light of the king, even in your thoughts. And don't make fun of a rich man, either. A little bird may tell them what you have said" (Ecclesiastes 10:20). Never underestimate the co-worker who is looking for an opportunity to ingratiate himself with the higher-ups. Have you ever been indiscreet in making comments about a superior and suffered the consequences? Explain what happened.

3. What was the most indiscreet conversation you have ever had, and what did you learn as a result?

4. Read Isaiah 39:1-8. What was King Hezekiah's indiscretion? What price did he pay for it?

5. Have you suffered any negative consequences as a result of someone else's indiscreet words? Please elaborate.

6. Read Genesis 9:20-25. What price did Ham pay for his indiscretion in how he exposed his father Noah's nakedness?

7. List at least three personal subjects that you as a discreet person *will not* discuss with anyone except a spouse or very close friend.

　　1.

　　2.

　　3.

8. Write out Proverbs 2:11 as a personal proclamation.

Scriptures to Ponder
for the Indiscreet Tongue

A word fitly spoken is like apples
of gold in settings of silver.
PROVERBS 25:11 NKJV

My son, pay attention to my wisdom;
listen carefully to my wise counsel.
Then you will learn to be discreet and will store up knowledge.
PROVERBS 5:1-2

Discretion is a life-giving fountain to those who possess it.
PROVERBS 16:22

A woman who is beautiful but lacks discretion is
like a gold ring in a pig's snout.
PROVERBS 11:22

Day 30

The Silent Tongue

While keeping silent is a virtue in some situations, if we want to be a voice for the voiceless, confront personal issues, and fight for justice, we are required to speak up. The key is to always use our voices for the right purpose, at the right time, and in the right manner.

1. Begin this lesson by reading Day 30, "The Silent Tongue," from your personal copy of *30 Days to Taming Your Tongue*. Note here at least one truth you found beneficial in your quest for a wholesome tongue.

2. Those who have not developed good communication skills or who do not understand the importance of effective confrontation will often resort to the silent treatment.

- Recall a time when you failed to confront an issue directly and chose to use your silence as a means of retaliation.

- Write a prayer of repentance for not handling the situation according to Matthew 18:15. In your prayer, include a plea for courage to communicate your hurts, desires, or preferences in a godly way.

3. List three circumstances noted in this chapter in which silence is not golden.

   1.

   2.

   3.

4. Describe a situation in which you spoke up on behalf of someone who could not (or was not present to) speak for himself. What were the results?

5. Recall a situation in which your silence implied you were in agreement with a certain course of action that you in fact opposed. What fears kept you from speaking up?

Scriptures to Ponder
for the Silent Tongue

Speak up for those who cannot speak for themselves;
ensure justice for those who are perishing.
Yes, speak up for the poor and helpless,
and see that they get justice.

PROVERBS 31:8-9

If your brother sins against you,
go and tell him his fault between you and him alone.
If he hears you, you have gained your brother.

MATTHEW 18:15 NKJV

There is a time for everything,
and a season for every activity under heaven…
a time to be silent and a time to speak.

ECCLESIASTES 3:1,7 NIV

Daily Tongue Evaluation Log

To measure your progress in taming your tongue, ask yourself the following questions at the end of each day. Indicate only your Yes ("Y") responses. For each Yes, meditate on the Scripture verses found in the related chapter of *30 Days to Taming Your Tongue*. Note any trends, and take them to the Lord in prayer.

	DAY OF THE MONTH	1	2	3	4	5
1	Did I engage in any form of lying (deceit, half-truth, exaggeration)?					
2	Did I attempt to flatter someone with an insincere compliment?					
3	Did I manipulate someone for my gain or advantage?					
4	Did I speak too hastily?					
5	Did my words cause division?					
6	Was I argumentative or contentious?					
7	Did I boast or speak with pride?					
8	Did I engage in a self put-down?					
9	Did I slander someone?					
10	Did I gossip?					
11	Did I meddle in anybody's affairs?					
12	Did I betray someone's trust?					
13	Did I belittle someone?					
14	Was I cynical, scornful, or sarcastic?					
15	Did I speak as a "know-it-all"?					
16	Did I use harsh or abusive words?					
17	Did I fail to speak with tact or diplomacy?					
18	Did I attempt to intimidate with my words?					
19	Was I rude?					
20	Was I critical or judgmental?					
21	Was I self-absorbed in my conversations?					
22	Did I use profanity?					
23	Did I complain?					
24	Did I retaliate?					
25	Did I accuse someone?					
26	Was I discouraging?					
27	Did I express doubt and unbelief?					
28	Did I simply talk too much?					
29	Was I indiscreet in my discussions?					
30	Did I keep silent when I should have spoken up?					

6	7	8	9	10	11	12	13	14	15	16	17	18	19	20	21	22	23	24	25	26	27	28	29	30

About the Author

Deborah Smith Pegues is an experienced certified public accountant, a Bible teacher, a speaker, and a certified behavioral consultant specializing in understanding personality temperaments. For Harvest House, she has authored *30 Days to Taming Your Tongue, 30 Days to Taming Your Finances, 30 Days to Taming Your Stress,* and *Conquering Insecurity.* She and her husband, Darnell, have been married for nearly 30 years and make their home in California.

For speaking engagements, please contact the author at...

The Pegues Group
P.O. Box 56382
Los Angeles, California 90056
(323) 293-5861
or
E-mail: ddpegues@sbcglobal.net
www.confrontingissues.com

Also by Deborah Smith Pegues,
available at www.confrontingissues.com:

Managing Conflict God's Way:
Biblical Strategies for Effective Confrontaitons

"Show Me the Money!":
Uncovering the Eight Pitfalls to Financial Freedom

HARVEST HOUSE
PUBLISHERS

Conquering Insecurity
Secrets to a More Confident You

Deborah Smith Pegues

*"A fresh, new, and exciting must-read book
that includes extraordinary wisdom."*

CONGRESSWOMAN DIANE E. WATSON

Is insecurity robbing you of life's fullness?

Conquering Insecurity uses biblical and modern-day examples to help you recognize and overcome insecurity's many guises. Strategies such as resting in God's Word, resisting intimidation, and remembering past victories provide an effective plan of attack on self-doubt. Beyond that, you'll discover how to put these key, life-changing concepts into action:

- valuing individuality

- establishing boundaries

- conquering perfectionism

- empowering others

- embracing success

You can understand and overcome the core fears that limit you. And you can build the confidence you need to enjoy life at home, at work, and at play!

*"Deborah Pegues presents simple but powerful strategies
for overcoming the sense of inadequacy that keeps many
from becoming the champions they were meant to be in life.
This work will coach you to victory!"*

EARVIN "MAGIC" JOHNSON,
FIVE-TIME NBA CHAMPION, ENTREPRENEUR

*"If you are having trouble making ends meet and wonder where
the money hole is, definitely pick this book up.
You won't be sorry—it might be the wisest $6 you've spent in years."*

30 Days to Taming Your Finances
What to Do (and Not Do) to Better Manage Your Money

Deborah Smith Pegues

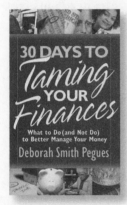

"How can I manage my money better?"

Have you ever thought how nice it would be to have an advisor at your side to help with financial decisions? Certified public accountant Deborah Pegues is an expert in money matters, and she has put together a simple, practical plan to help you rein in unruly spending habits and find peace and plenty in your pocket in 30 days.

With transparency about her own financial mistakes and a bit of refreshing sass, Deborah devotes easy-to-follow chapters to help you learn how to...

- diminish your debt
- spend smart
- save strategically
- profit from your passion
- further your financial intelligence
- and start 25 more finance-taming habits

Anecdotes, soul-searching questions, and biblical principles combine to make each chapter full of hope that a healthy and satisfying financial future is about to be a dream come true.

30 Days to Taming Your Stress
Deborah Smith Pegues

"How do I control stress instead of letting it control me?"

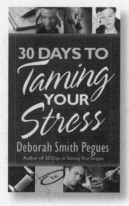

Are you sleeping well at night? Finding enough time in the day to do the things you enjoy? Making good choices about food and exercise? Sometimes stress causes us to miss out on the rest, fun, and health we long for. But you truly can tame this unruly taskmaster in 30 short days.

With insight gleaned from her experience as a behavioral consultant, bestselling author Deborah Smith Pegues devotes stress-free chapters to help you learn how to...

- change self-sabotaging behavior

- enjoy the present

- evaluate your expectations

- release your tension

- solidify your support system

- and begin 25 more stress-taming habits

Personal anecdotes, soul-searching questions, and biblical principles combine to make each chapter full of practical ways to help you stress less and enjoy life more in a remarkably short time.

*"In her trademark direct and engaging style,
Deborah shares powerful strategies for responding
to and reducing your stress."*

PAULA WHITE
PASTOR, LIFE COACH, MOTIVATIONAL SPEAKER